World of Engineering

Making a Computer

Natalie Humphrey

PowerKiDS press

Published in 2024 by The Rosen Publishing Group, Inc.
2544 Clinton Street, Buffalo, NY 14224

Portions of this work were originally authored by Sam Aloian and published as *How a Computer Is Built.* All new material in this edition was authored by Natalie Humphrey.

Editor: Natalie Humphrey
Designer: Rachel Rising

Photo Credits: Cover, Africa Studio/Shutterstock.com; Cover, pp. 1-24 Alef-Beth/Shutterstock.com; Cover, pp. 1-24 Artistdesign29/Shutterstock.com; Cover, pp. 1, 3, 22-24 RoseRodionova/Shutterstock.com; Cover, p. 1 Creative Hawk/Shutterstock.com; p. 5 Daniel Chetroni/Shutterstock.com; p. 6 AmazeinDesign/Shutterstock.com; p. 7 Syafiq Adnan/Shutterstock.com; p. 9 Naumov S/Shutterstock.com; p. 10 anmbph/Shutterstock.com; p. 11 FeelGoodLuck/Shutterstock.com; p. 13 daniiD/Shutterstock.com; p. 14 ubonwanu/Shutterstock.com; p. 15 Hadrian/Shutterstock.com; p. 17 Aleksandr Grechanyuk/Shutterstock.com; p. 19 Preechar Bowonkitwanchai/Shutterstock.com; pp. 20, 21 Yasir Design/Shutterstock.com; p. 20 Gorodenkoff/Shutterstock.com; p. 20, 21 ZinetroN/Shutterstock.com; p. 21 Deemerwha studio/Shutterstock.com; p. 21 Monkey Business Images/Shutterstock.com.

Author: Humphrey, Natalie.
Title: Making a computer / Natalie Humphrey.
Description: Buffalo, New York : Powerkids Press, 2024. | Series: World of engineering | Includes index, glossary, and bibliographic information
Identifiers: ISBN 9781642826432 (pbk) | ISBN 9781642826449 (library bound) | ISBN 9781642826456 (ebook)
Subjects: LCSH: Computer science-- Juvenile literature | Engineering--Juvenile literature | Technology--Juvenile literature
Classification: LCC TK7885.5 H86 2024 | DDC 004--dc24

Manufactured in the United States of America

CPSIA Compliance Information: Batch #CSPK24. For Further Information contact Rosen Publishing at 1-800-237-9932.

CONTENTS

COMPUTERS EVERYWHERE!

While they don't always look alike, computers are all around us. Some computers are small, such as the ones inside tablets and cellphones. Some giant computers, called supercomputers, are big enough to take up an entire room.

Every year, the technology inside computers improves. Today's computers are much faster than early computers. Even though computers have changed, the way computers are put together is still similar. So how are computers made? Let's find out!

ENGINEERING WONDERS

People who **design** the parts of a computer are called hardware engineers. These are people who plan and build machines. People who design the **programs** used on a computer are called software engineers.

TINY COMPUTERS, SUCH AS THE RASPBERRY PI BELOW, HAVE MANY OF THE SAME PARTS AS LARGER COMPUTERS.

One of the most common types of computers is called a desktop. The main hardware of a computer is usually inside a computer case. This is called a system unit. The system unit is connected to a screen called a monitor which shows what the computer is doing.

Users use input devices, or tools that are made to perform a task, to tell the computer what to do. Keyboards are used to type letters and a computer's mouse **interacts** with objects shown on the monitor.

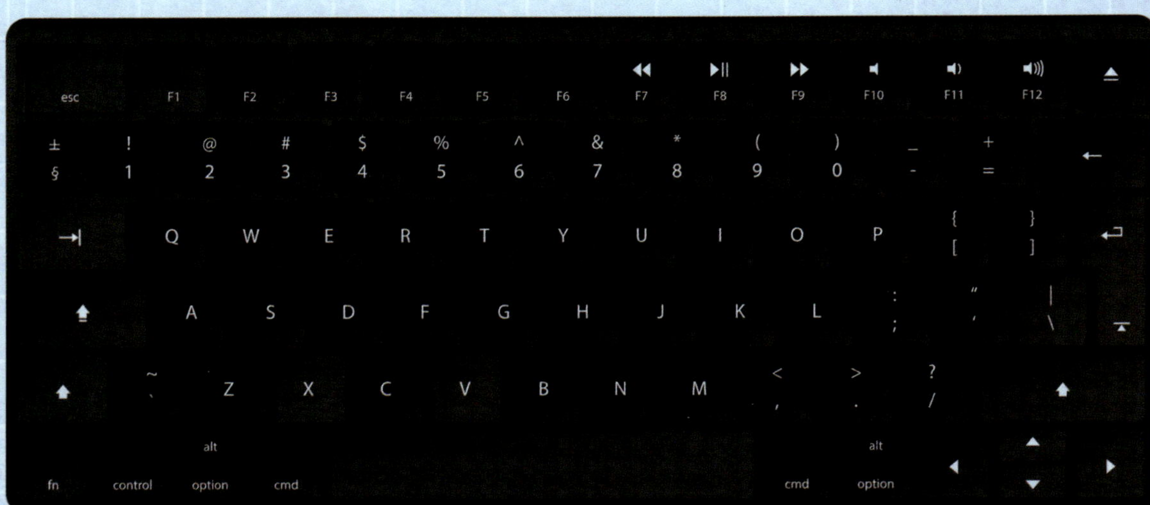

ENGINEERING WONDERS

A computer's OS, or **operating system**, helps the computer run. Windows, Linux, and macOS are all different types of operating systems.

INPUT DEVICES HELP THE USER TELL THE COMPUTER WHAT TO DO.

THE MOTHERBOARD

There are many different parts inside a system unit that help the computer run. Sometimes, workers assemble, or put together, these parts in a factory. Many people build their own computers at home as well!

The first pieces to go into the computer case are the motherboard and CPU (Central **Processing** Unit). The motherboard connects all the parts of the computer to the CPU. The CPU acts like the brain of the computer and tells the other parts what to do.

ENGINEERING WONDERS

When a CPU is working, it can get very hot. The average CPU temperature is between 104 and 149°F (40 and 65°C), but it can be hotter than 176°F (80°C)!

MOTHERBOARDS, LIKE THE ONE BELOW, COME IN MANY DIFFERENT COLORS, SHAPES, AND SIZES.

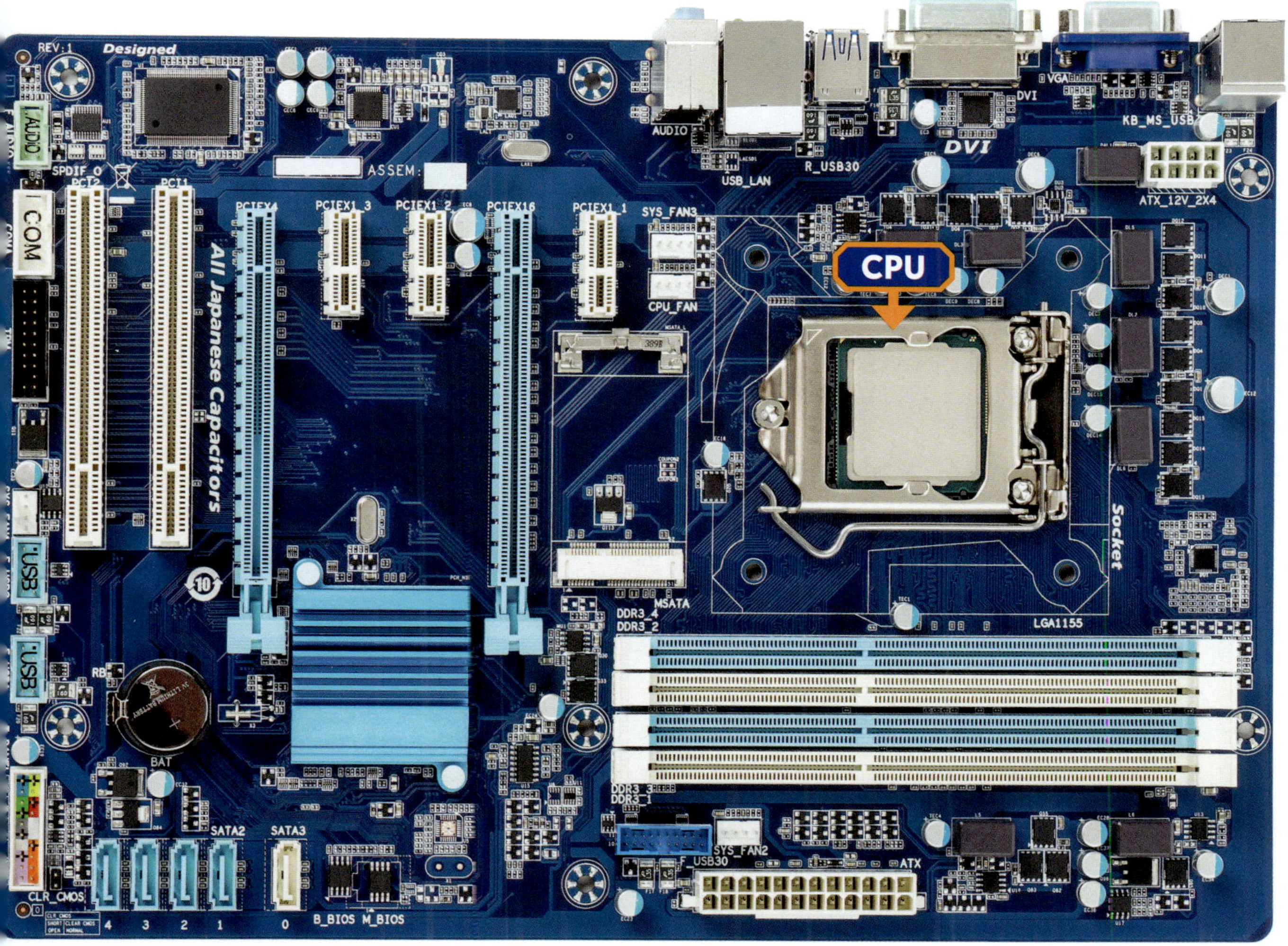

Cooling is an important part of building a computer. Because a CPU gets so hot, they need fans to keep from overheating, or becoming too hot. After the builder puts a fan onto the CPU, they connect the computer to a power source and test it.

A computer's power source is called a power supply. Power supplies connect the computer to a power outlet in your home. The power supply has many wires that **insert** into the different devices in the computer.

ENGINEERING WONDERS

Fans aren't the only way to cool a CPU. Some computers use **liquid** cooling. This type of cooling uses **pumps** and a special kind of liquid to keep the computer cool.

TO CONNECT THE CPU FAN TO THE CPU, BUILDERS USE A PASTE CALLED **THERMAL COMPOUND**.

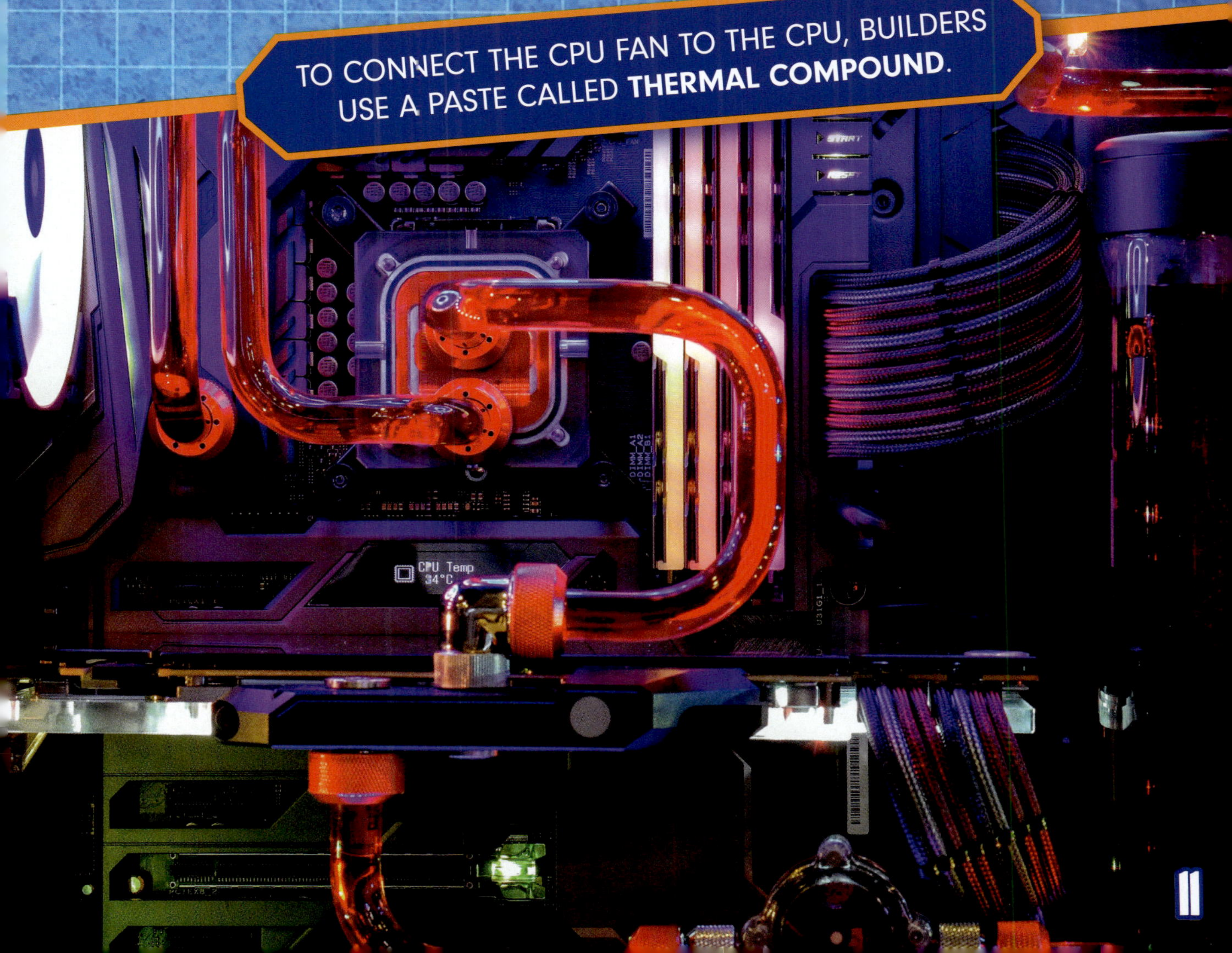

THE COMPUTER'S MEMORY

After the CPU and motherboard, it's time to **install** the memory. The memory of the computer is also called RAM. RAM is where the CPU keeps information, or knowledge and facts about something, until the computer is turned off. When you turn the computer off, this information is gone!

RAM comes in pairs, or sets of two. Builders push the pairs into spots on the motherboard next to the CPU. The RAM needs to be inserted in a certain way to work correctly.

ENGINEERING WONDERS

There are many kinds of RAM, but not all work with every kind of motherboard! Engineers need to make sure they're using the right kind of memory for the computer they're building.

MOST MOTHERBOARDS HAVE FOUR SLOTS FOR RAM.

Hard drives are another form of computer memory. Hard drives store memory even when the computer is turned off. The computer's OS, programs, and other important information are stored on a hard drive. The hard drive is connected to the motherboard so other hardware can **communicate** with the hard drive.

There are two different types of hard drives. Hard disk drives (HDD) use magnets to save memory to a spinning disk. Solid-state drives (SSD) are smaller and save information to a thin element that doesn't move.

ENGINEERING WONDERS

Instead of using wires, some newer motherboards have a spot for an SSD to be put in directly.

SSDS WORK MUCH FASTER THAN MOST HDDS.

THE GRAPHICS CARD

After connecting the hard drive, it's time to install the **graphics** card. The graphics card is what connects the motherboard to the monitor. Some graphics cards are built into the motherboard. Faster and larger graphics cards are usually separate cards.

Most graphics cards have a GPU attached to them. A GPU, just like a CPU, helps the graphics card process information. The faster the GPU, the faster the computer can put images on the monitor.

ENGINEERING WONDERS

You'll need faster graphics cards to run videos or play video games smoothly. Many newer games need a faster graphics card to run at all!

MORE POWERFUL GRAPHICS CARDS OFTEN HAVE FANS CONNECTED TO THEM.

FINAL TESTS

After installing all the parts, the builder can test the computer again. These tests are to make sure everything is connected and running the way it should. If the computer passes these tests, the builder can close the case and install the OS and other software.

In factories, workers test the computer one more time to make sure they installed the software properly. If everything is working correctly, the computer is ready to be sold!

ENGINEERING WONDERS

Some companies will let users customize, or change to fit someone's tastes, what goes into their computer before it's even built.

IF YOU WERE BUILDING A COMPUTER, WHAT WOULD YOU PUT INSIDE?

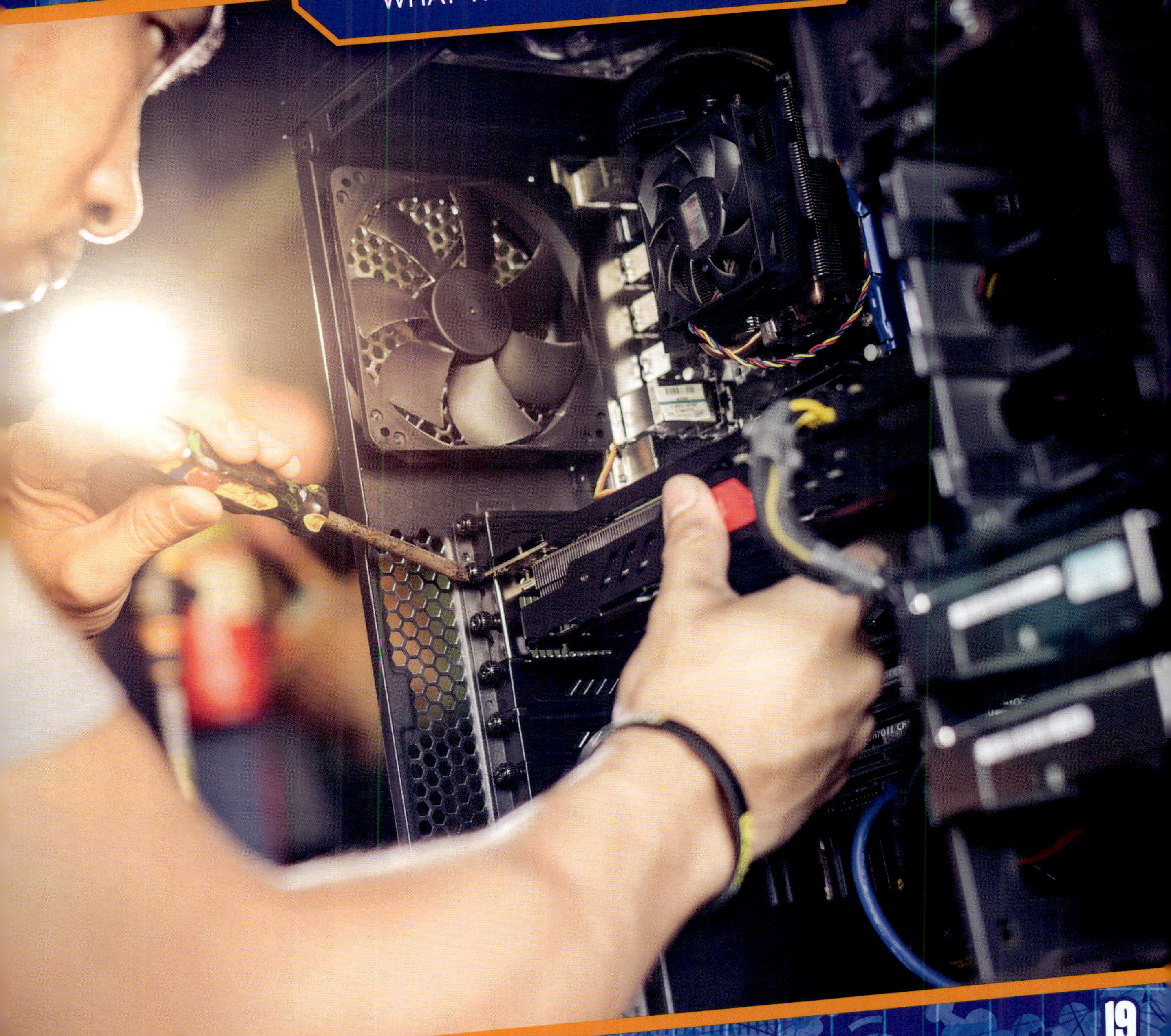

CODING LIKE A SOFTWARE ENGINEER

Building your own computer can be expensive. If you already have a computer though, you can code like a software engineer instead! Here are some websites you can visit to try out computer coding yourself.

tynker.com

tynker.com

Tynker helps you make your own video games, program a robot, and do much more!

kidsruby.com

kidsruby.com

Ruby is a fun programming language you can use to make all kinds of things.

GLOSSARY

communicate: To share knowledge or information.

design: To create the pattern or shape of something.

graphics: The images, designs, or drawings that are displayed on a screen.

insert: To put something into something else.

install: To set something up to be used.

interact: To come together and have an effect on each other.

liquid: Something that flows and takes the shape of the container holding it.

operating system: The program a computer uses to control other programs.

process: A series of steps or actions taken to complete something.

program: A piece of computer code that tells a computer what to do.

pump: A machine that forces liquid through a hose.

thermal compound: A thick paste made of different matter and used to pull heat away from the CPU.

FOR MORE INFORMATION

BOOKS

Borgert-Spaniol, Megan. *Invent a Game!: and More Coding & Strategy Challenges.* Minneapolis, MN: Super Sandcastle, 2021.

Fromowitz, Lori. *Building a Computer.* Lake Elmo, MN: Focus Reachers, 2020.

WEBSITES

CodaKid
www.codakid.com/parts-of-a-computer/
Learn more about the different parts inside a computer.

Raspberry Pi Foundation
www.projects.raspberrypi.org/en
Find out how you can make your own devices with Raspberry Pi parts.

INDEX